anagnorisis

5
H/22

Also by Kyle Dargan

Honest Engine (2015)

KINGSLEY TUFTS POETRY AWARD FINALIST AND
HURSTON/WRIGHT LEGACY AWARD FINALIST

Logorrhea Dementia (2010)

Bouquet of Hungers (2007)

HURSTON/WRIGHT LEGACY AWARD WINNER

The Listening (2004)

CAVE CANEM POETRY PRIZE WINNER

Anagnorisis

Poems

KYLE Dargan

 TRIQUARTERLY BOOKS/NORTHWESTERN UNIVERSITY PRESS

Northwestern University Press
www.nupress.northwestern.edu

Printed in the United States of America

10 9 8 7 6 5 4 3 2 1

ISBN 978-0-8101-3784-4 (paper)
ISBN 978-0-8101-3785-1 (ebook)

Cataloging-in-Publication Data are available from the Library of Congress.

for Kaede—

a glimmer cresting the edge of an enduring night

If you are a citizen, why do you have to fight for your civil rights? If you're fighting for your civil rights, that means you're not a citizen.
—JAMES BALDWIN

> The answer to the riddle is me,
> and here's the question: who can be . . .
> —DOVE

Acknowledgments   *xi*

Dark Humor

Failed Sonnet after the Verdict   5

Avenger   6

Daily Conscription   7

White. Bread. Blues.   9

Olympic / Drive   10

Looking East as a Man Repairs Lights on the South Street Pier   12

Beauty   14

Poem Resisting Arrest   17

Death Toll   19

Eastland   20

The Economy of Swallowed Knives   22

La Petite Mort   24

Dave Chappelle Confuses George Washington with Thomas Jefferson   26

It's Possible I'm Too Bougie to Be Free   28

Americana   31

In 2016, the African-American Poet Kyle Dargan Is Asked to Consider Writing More Like the African-American Poet Ross Gay   34

Another Poem Beginning with a Bullet   40

Distances

Lost One   45

I Too   48

China Cycle

I. Economy Class	53
II. Dilemma in Comparison	54
III. Body Binhai	55
V. A Progressive Mile	57
VII. Ni, Wo	59
IX. The Way of Intersections	60
X. The Shouts of Tanggu Station	61
XI. "Beautiful Country"	62
XII. Early Onset Survivor's Guilt	64
XV. Voices on the River	65
XVI. The Wooden Phoenix at Ling Tong	66
XX. Da Shuo	68
XXI. Meal at Pyongyang	69
XXII. Devils Have No Fans	71

Dear Echo

Natural Causes	75
Sublimation	76
Separating	78
Generation Kindling	80
Tredegar	82
Thirty-Four	83
The Darkening	84
Dear Echo	86
Recognition	89
Notes	91

ACKNOWLEDGMENTS

Earlier versions of some of the poems in this book were originally published in the following venues:

Academy of American Poets Poem-a-Day: "Daily Conscription"

American Poetry Review: "Avenger," "The Darkening," "Dave Chappelle Confuses George Washington with Thomas Jefferson," "Death Toll"

Beltway Poetry Quarterly: "Failed Sonnet after the Verdict," "It's Possible I'm Too Bougie to Be Free"

District Lit: "Eastland"

Four Way Review: "Beauty," "The Economy of Swallowed Knives"

Grist: "Generation Kindling," "Thirty-Four"

Gulf Coast: "Another Poem Beginning with a Bullet"

jubilat: "Da Shuo"

No, Dear (Black Poets Speak Out): "Poem Resisting Arrest"

Pleiades: "Tredegar"

Palette Poetry: "Sublimation"

Poetry: "Dear Echo," "Olympic / Drive"

Public Pool: "La Petite Mort," "White. Bread. Blues."

The Rumpus: "Americana"

The Saint Ann's Review: "Economy Class," "Meal at Pyongyang"

Tin House: "In 2016, the African-American Poet Kyle Dargan Is Asked to Consider Writing More Like the African-American Poet Ross Gay"

West Branch: "The Way of Intersections"

"Beautiful Country" and "Looking East as a Man Repairs Lights on the South Street Pier" appeared in *Read America(s): An Anthology*, published by Locked Horn Press.

"Natural Causes" was originally published as one of Split This Rock's Poem of the Week features and is archived in its social justice poetry database The Quarry. The poem also appeared in the anthology *Bullets into Bells: Poets and Citizens Respond to Gun Violence,* published by Beacon Press.

"Americana" appeared in *Misrepresented People: Poetic Responses to Trump's America,* published by NYQ Books.

Anagnorisis

dark humor

You all know how black humor started? It started in the slave
ships, you know? Cat was on his way over here, rowing. Another
dude said, "What you laughing about?" He said, "Yesterday,
I was a king."

—RICHARD PRYOR

FAILED SONNET AFTER THE VERDICT

I have begun, one month since, to actually believe
only George Zimmerman screamed behind that 911 call.
It burns less when I assume George better understood
this arena, knew how to exhale race and scent our air
so that history's winds would record any shrill plea
as his own—as the terror of a brown man overwhelmed,

not the terror of a deeper brown Trayvon. I don't believe
the gun, its firing, was hateful. Zimmerman I find guilty
of collusion: dredging up the cotton gin fan's gothic maw,
yoking it to another child devoured. Self-defense: George
sank them beneath a blood river, a preordained drowning.
No jury exists for such execution. Again, under this State,
angst absolves the trigger finger shaken by we
shadows—a silencing of our hearts' transgressive beat.

AVENGER

Behind 1600's gates, the President sits bound
to the presidency like a superhero sidekick,
his mouth gagged by what "originalists" believe
the constitution says. Live streams, meanwhile,
pump night-green footage from Ferguson's
punctured lung into our timelines. Flash
grenades gush like stars spangling from a flag
drawn and quartered. I feel a vicarious
smallness watching demonstrators flee.
A boy has been murdered again. Again,
an officer has judged a body's rising, or
darkening, as having breached the threshold
    of *menace*
      (*demon*)—   needing to be put down.
Rage would be a word to fit in the mouth
had the mouth not grown small from watching
SWAT tanks quash demands for answers.
The Attorney General—just a brown man reclined
on a couch—watches it all and grows impatient
with due process. Somewhere, at his beckoning,
his Iron Man suit rises from some silo—rocketing
towards his home, where he'll armor up then fly
over to Missouri and repel riot cops
whose tear gas fogs residential streets.
Somewhere is the negro's imagined America,
where we have Iron Man on our side,
though it does not matter if the hero is "black"
so long as the body inside is. But super suits
and costumes don't function like the Oval
Office. Vote a "black" man into a white house.
It's still the White House—symbol of everything
we've been escaping—not a beacon, never rescue.

DAILY CONSCRIPTION

We can no longer afford that particular romance.
—JAMES BALDWIN

Brother Rickey halts me before I cross East
Capitol. He trumpets that we are at war.

I want to admit that I don't believe in "white"
—in the manner that Baldwin did not—but Brother

Rickey would simply retort that my disbelief
is no immunity from the imaginations of those

who think themselves "white." As we await
the stoplight's shift—so I may walk and he may

holler "Final Call!" between lanes of idle traffic—
I think of race as something akin to climate change,

a force we don't have to believe in for it to undo us.
I once believed in the seasons. (I fantasize

fall as Brother Rickey's favorite—when his suits,
boxy and plaid, would be neither too hot nor

thin.) But we are losing spring and fall—tripping
from blaze to frost and back. And what's to say

we won't soon shed another season, one of these
remaining two, and live on either an Earth

of molten streets or one of frozen light? That's when
worlds end, no—when, after we've eradicated

ourselves, we become faint fossils to be exhumed
by the curiosities of whichever life-forms follow

our reign? I still owe Brother Rickey two dollars
for the paper he last placed in my hand, calling me

"soldier." I don't have to believe that I am enlisted
in order to understand he'll forgive my debt

so long as this idea of "whiteness" sorties above us—
ultraviolet, obliging an aseasonal, unending deployment.

Released by the signal, I advance—my head down,
straining to discern the crossfire from the cover.

WHITE. BREAD. BLUES.

The Islander on U Street will be shuttered
says the metro section of the *Washington Post*.
I had my first and last plate of their curry bird
after Heroes Are Gang Leaders hit at Howard.
Can I be sad? I think I've made my peace
with gentrification. I tell myself, *market value*
all it is—not race. Then there is no bitter
echo within my skull. Georgia Avenue—Shaw
on up to Florida Avenue—these days
glimmers with *eateries* and *wellness studios*.
Donnie Simpson's son owns a bakery
atop the metro. That's music. That's
America, I guess. I stopped somewhere
for a sandwich—which is why I am writing
this poem. Maybe gentrification
is dropping thirteen dollars for some catfish
on brioche that tastes too sweet
and lacks the structural integrity of whatever
hard-fried fare you could carry from the dingy
storefronts that dared to make a dollar when
the afterbirth of riots was all that clung
upon these streets. I tried walking and eating
but a tempura catfish sandwich shakes to bits
when you pass in front of Howard University
Hospital, where all the healed bamas bop
out the doors styled like Batman villains
if Gotham was Detroit instead of Manhattan—
their skins embroidered with question marks.
Everyone needs a place to be strange, or a city
where you know what will and won't leave you
hungry.

OLYMPIC / DRIVE

Across from the gorgeous dog park,
men dream against poodle-pissed trees—
their pillows crafted from breath captured
in milk cartons. Only arid, temperate
climate offers respite. Let us suppose
they too have tales, here in this city
where filmed stories turn a mint.
All around, one wide screen—the dark hills
due north pixel-pocked with villa lights.
Below, streets hemmed with haggard
brown men—jack-in-the-box bodies
ever unfolding. Who is pitching
this script? Title: "The Child of 1968."
Voiceover: *After the Integration Apocalypse,*
one man must find his way in a land
where the sole survivors who look or speak
like him are those rendered deranged
and indigent. Assume the Motion Picture
Association eager to levy a "Rated R,"
then remember that those who judge
violence never shared your definition
of savagery. A culling is all your eyes
decipher—your herd thinned. No urban
wildlife anywhere to be found,
yet hunger for a hunt remains.
Tagline: *A hero must choose—*
between starving or bartering one's own
skin. Plot: *Amid the solar famine, bio-*
electric research has revealed melanin's
subtle charge—the brown population gone
mad from being sapped like CopperTops.

Imagine The Matrix *without the extra-*
terrestrial machines. Imagine that among us
have lived scientists churning statistics,
devising a human harvest, a controlled carnage
to subsist off fellow men. The drained bones
left to be gnawed by next century's hounds.

LOOKING EAST AS A MAN REPAIRS LIGHTS ON THE SOUTH STREET PIER

> *I too lived—Brooklyn, of ample hills, was mine*
> —WALT WHITMAN

Who are these who teem in, who have taken,
the borough of trees? From this perch,
I struggle to identify them—these new who now
colonize the sprawling gray out there, well south
of this busy brown river's far bank.

So many buildings have been wrecked
(via ball, via jet) since I spent odd afternoons
as a boy upon this pier, waiting for water's
interpretation of our lives. (We being majority
water, I assumed a river might know.)

       Still, the shadow of the bridge
and Whitman's words make a humble shroud.
If not the world's, at least this nation's
meaning spoke clearest to me here—
under the iron, limestone, and granite span
twenty-seven men perished to erect.

Ellis Island wades downriver
somewhere we cannot see nor remember.
Crossing, constant crossing.
Cross or be crossed. No malice in that—
either you're crossing a line in this land
or becoming the line to be traversed.

       Between the pier
and the water, only a railing. An electrician
hooks his harness to the metal, then hops
over the side to replace fizzled lights.

He frets falling into the river—losing
his place in this country.

      He knows
the boundaries we've imagined, we've drawn,
hold no authority beneath the water
—its undulating disregard for cartographer's
ink that we are convinced defines us.

BEAUTY

Miss Iraq, the first   crowned

     in forty years of foreign meddling,

means it when she wishes for world peace—

     her cousins' deaths

both tallied   by sectarian violence in her

war-quilted, war-torn nation.

     She is aware

the pageantry—   parade smiles and stiff,

cupped hands (their rotational gesture)

—will not beckon peace.   Salvation

     may have functioned

such ways in old, dog-eared eras. There's evidence:

all our parched frescoes or weathered statues

     depicting one or another stoic god,

     its crimped hand raised,

signaling for peace like a captain calling a play.

Run peace, they might have said,

or *run samsara*   or *run godhead*

if peace is too transparent a trick

name for an offensive set.   In Saddam City,

today, broken men train to play

the beautiful game, to execute levity

with their feet. Under Hussein's boot,

losses on the pitch would translate

into torture—forty degrees Celsius

sessions training to kick   molded concrete

futbols or hours

spent begging deliverance from within

an iron maiden's spiked void. Those years

we call "the dark era"—when Saddam's son,

Mr. Uday, was the face

of Iraq's Olympic committee,

before he would become the ace of hearts

in the most-wanted card decks

coalition troops carried in their fatigues.

"Clearly recognisable"   —how the *Guardian*

would describe Uday

Hussein in U.S.-released glamour shots—

    "despite having a thick beard

and a wound   that had destroyed

part of his nose and upper lip."

                On this side

of that suffering,   five years since

Iraqi Freedom's end,

Ms. Qasim will wear the red,

    green, and black sash,

and the U-23 team will play

for Olympic glory, despite the death

threats that may bloom into wails.

Authority's lens abhors

    beauty—its saturation in this world,

its disregard for the vacuums

men slaughter each other to create.

POEM RESISTING ARREST

This poem will be guilty. It assumed it retained
the right to ask its question after the page

came up flush against its face. The purpose
this poem serves is obvious, even to this poem,

and that cannot stop the pen or the fist
choking it. How the page tastes at times—unsalted

powerlessness in this poem's mouth, a blend
of that and what news the poem has swallowed. It spits

blood—inking. It is its own doing and undoing.
This poem is trying to compose itself. It has

the right to remain either bruised or silent,
but it is a poem, so it hears *you'd be safer*

if you stopped acting like a poem, ceased resisting.
Where is the daylight (this poem asks and is

thus crushed) between existence and resistance,
between the now-bloodied page and the poem?

Another poem will record the arrest of this poem,
decide what to excerpt. That poem will fail—

it won't find the right metaphor for the pain
of having to lift epigraphs from the closing

words of poems that were accused of resisting.
That poem is numb. This poem is becoming

numb, already losing feeling in its cuffed phrasing.
No one will remember the nothing of which

this poem was accused—just that it was another
poem that bled. This poem never expected to be

this poem, yet it must be—for you who will not
acknowledge the question. This poem knew

it was dangerous to ask *why?*

DEATH TOLL

> *Somehow, this has become routine.*
> —BARACK OBAMA

This road has surely paid for itself by now,
but let's toss some more bullets in the bucket.

Clipped bodies pile up, obscuring the medians,
where we toss our spare bullets in the bucket.

Roll down the window. Eye a distant monument
to war. Let new deaths in the foreground blur.

Wasn't it Eisenhower who aimed to hasten our arms
course across the country—barrels roving interstate air?

This news smears against our windshields again
and we'll toss still-warm bullets into the bucket.

Spent rounds sink over the blood-brimming rim,
burying names that line the bottom of the bucket.

EASTLAND

*Son, you know what it is
from the moment you come over the bridge.*
—YASIIN BEY

Where the sun first rises, that is where
I savor our somber, our dark—
how it unsettles acquaintances
visiting this Dee Cee
from across the Anacostia, from Washington.

Absent the downtown static—
the jostling fenders, the tapping
thumbs of young professionals newly wedded
to work—absent that scratching,
there is, out here, a quiet so crisp
I can hear the two-mile echo of each
rust-heeled freight train and gunshot.

It's *peaceful*, meaning I can isolate
the sounds as dollars chase dollars
or as rib cages catch bullets
—everything else just trying to rest.

If I describe Southeast as *sleepy*, don't you
correct me—especially if fear has whittled
your eyes into prisms, and you see
this adjacent eastward landscape as overrun
with untrained triggers and hands
that squeeze and thieve.

Our bleeding is not random. At nightfall,
we are not here awaiting a chance to stalk
the whites nesting your dilating irises.

We have our own private violence to stir
and sip just like you—most often
not on the streets but inside our own homes.

This quiet so plush, it would be no
surprise to learn that they could hear it
here when Marvin Gaye, who first soprano'd
and shimmied just off East Capitol,
took two point-blank slugs
from a .38 he'd bought his father,
in a house he'd bought his father—
that holy high note reaching
all the way from LA, 4:01 P.M. EST,
before his pulse flattened into a horizon.

THE ECONOMY OF SWALLOWED KNIVES

I warn an auditorium full of children,
Do not try this at home. Then I begin
ingesting skewers. Without intent,
I enlist their bright-eyed volition
into the war against waiting to grow up.

On the drive home, they pelt their parents
with salvos of *Can I* and *Please*, while fathers,
being fathers, retort, *When you're grown,*
paying your own bills for your own roof,
you'll be free to live as foolhardily as your heart
desires. There: the moment of escalation—

suddenly their every waking hour becomes
a struggle to buy back their right to self-
destruction. Lemonade stands and lawn
mowing. Frozen meat pucks flipped
under sallowed arches, endless refolding
of denim. The children sprout acne and fuzz
as their piggy banks pudge. Their minds
have long since forgotten the death-defying
blade sleight that followed my disclaimer
years ago.

       They are teenagers. Everywhere
something else shouts *This could kill you,*
and, achingly, they answer *Yes.* They can
taste it: tattoos, cigarettes, and sex—
any form of flirting with mortality.
Beneath youth's aegis, they believe
themselves mighty, no matter how poor,
but soon enough they are adults renting
efficiencies and driving jalopies—stretching
dimes for the privilege of being *grown.*

See how this economy needed no help
in tailoring their malaise? And what next?
Heat assignments for the middle-class
scramble to obfuscate death.
Then kids of their own. Then the rest.

LA PETITE MORT

goal for today / the rest of my life: weaponize happiness.
—FATIMAH ASGHAR

Many of us are here today because it is difficult
to maneuver when experiencing an orgasm.

My friend, responding to his girlfriend's laments
about their second infant, shouted "well, I told you

to get off of me." It was a futile warning.
The boy is, god knows, how many years old now.

Life goes on. That is the point—after the little death,
life goes on. We live in a world of Tasers,

of tranquilizer darts and anesthesia. By accident,
these kill us on occasion. That big death—

the one from which none have returned, wherein
your flesh seizes, clams, but never reanimates.

Then there are the guns which . . . well, I cannot explain
guns beyond the intent to call forth the big death.

But if all we need is a means to slow or subdue
people, why not give the police orgasm guns?

Whose legs churn fluidly while the brain is taken
by a stampede of endorphins? Who is a *threat*

with spastic genitals? I am reimaging the past
four years. Rather than queues of choppy footage

in which men and women are deaded
point-blank by the police, I see bodies

buckling and dropping to the pavement,
mouths gushing expletives though none in pain.

The cops could even shoot the Caucasian killers
who they infrequently shoot. They would still live

to be later gassed or injected to death—
which we call a *penalty*, a process much slower

than what skips over judgment to execution,
bursts premature through the thoraxes of brown

people. I cannot afford to believe that someday
the State, these states, will stop shooting my cousins,

so let there be another weapon—one that induces
only the small death. Yes, my cousins would come

against their wills, but they would come back,
unlike this big leaving—this spasm without release.

DAVE CHAPPELLE CONFUSES GEORGE WASHINGTON
WITH THOMAS JEFFERSON

Yes, I said it—though he has said wrong. *The worst*
                                                    of the worst:

naming the Father who hunted
                    runagates, broke families
by selling fathers back to the West Indies,
and fractured wills with threats of trade.
We mythologize this motherfucker who apprehended
"my countrymen will expect too much from me."
                                                    We like him

because he wrote the Declaration
of Independence and that shit,
                            but that was another
Virginian, another Virginia—supposedly
just as torn as George: Thomas. What matter, though,
the matching of names and slaver pasts to Chappelle,
who descends from the chatteled,   who has inherited
the labor of distilling humor from this bloody malt?

                    Our history—when made
                    funny—we remember,
resulting inaccuracies and all. For comedy's sake,
For What It's Worth, Dave conflates
our Fathers—one evoked for his storied reluctance
and one we idolize for his viciousness
with the pen. The irony of liberty's
                    violence is the punch line—

the soon-to-be first leader of the free
world embarked from Mount Vernon
        with the nauseous pangs of a "culprit
who is going to the place of his execution."

Washington, in his will, decreed his "Slaves"
freed upon the death of his widowed love.
Martha released them the year George was buried
—worried those men and women might deduce
all that remained of their servitude was her grave-
                                        bound body.
She feared the violence
carved into their skin   ("We hold
would dispel the violence   (these truths to be

embroidered on their minds.   (self-evident—
                                  (all men are created equal . . ."

That was 1800—the states in precarious unity—but such a fear
remains, at best, laughable.

                    (Go get me a sandwich, nigger,
                    (or I'll kill you . . . "Liberty and Justice
                    (for all."

IT'S POSSIBLE I'M TOO BOUGIE TO BE FREE

My peoples keep messaging me,

        attaching pig roast

            invites that request my presence

when the skewered hog will baste

        in juices of its own,

            of signifying & laughter. In this new-

new century, we have left behind us

        the so-called plantation

            cuisine. Kale's green claws

now grip the American palate (just

        as they've always enchanted

            our grandmothers' unsung pots &

recipes). Yet I'm worried I'm missing

        a hint—that *pig roast*

            might be code secluding the rally

point where hearts & hands knead

        a strategy for education

            reform, where blk wealth's meager

carcass is stewed & stretched, ladled

        onto plates faced with Fannie

            Lou Hamer or Baldwin or Malcolm

X. I want a plate (in theory), but I don't

want to wade into pork's

        social awkwardness, to risk being asked

what's wrong? What—you think you

        too good? This meat

        that saturated my elders' hearts—

making of their lives incomplete

        meals. I know code

        switching. I know how a song

do & don't tell. I'm tired of talking

        too. I want in on

        a dark revolt that swings low

or sneaks up on Uncle Sam like high

        blood pressure. It is

        possible coincidence accounts

for these cellular pings alerting me

        when another pig

        will be undressed by flame.

Food zealots deem swine the *it*

        protein but maybe we gut,

        we roast, the pig as idolatry.

They are sharp animals. Their noses

        can pierce seven

        miles of air for a morsel's scent

or unearth roots & tubers

like backhoes. Their minds

        catalog the ingredients of their own

faces, as well as the eyes & auras

        of others—biped or quad

            —in their memories. Emotionally keener

than the cats & dogs so many shelter

        as family. All that prowess,

            yet most pigs live & die penned in steel

quarters no broader than their bodies.

        I have tasted constriction.

        I know the spirit may be liberated

through fire. Maybe I want to be

        hog-led to freedom.

        Remember, what sizzles on the spit

—heart, chitterlings, & hog maw

        removed—is no longer

        the pig. The pig is rutting celestial

soil full parsecs into the future,

        foraging for truffles—north

        stars—it can taste but cannot see.

AMERICANA

The last thing my vision grazes
                    ahead a red-eye
                    London departure—

Obama's smiling face on toilet paper
                    rolls pyramid-stacked
                    at the gift shop

entryway. This is Washington Dulles
                    in his final year atop
                    a tiring administration.

I lost a good friend over the vote
                    this country cast
                    in 2008. She believed

the moment to be revolutionary. I dissented
                    that no radical seed
                    had taken root

on our soil. Had I known she and I
                    would—over that—
                    wither as friends,

I could have feigned exuberance, imitated
                    upheaval. Now, nagging
                    unemployment

statistics have since been tamed, as well as
                    the white numbers
                    between the dollar sign

and the gallon. Nevertheless, eight years later,
                    some things—some friendships—
                    have not been restored.

And yet, you do not see me wishing for the means
                    with which to scour
                    the President's grayscale face

against my anus. The postwipe sarcasm—*Thanks,*
                    Obama—as a gesture
                    of the body

cleansing the body. Though didn't he run
                    to clean and change
                    a soiled nation's bottom?

And even that, the privilege of allowing
                    someone else
                    to wipe your ass,

this country could not receive from his brown
                    hand housed
                    in a white glove.

Twice, I have gripped this President's bare hand—
                    America's shit pressed
                    against my palm—

and asked him, silently *was it worth it?* Tonight,
                    I cross the Atlantic
                    having lost

my antecedent for that *it*. Maybe just eight
                    years of static. A ratcheting
                    whir akin to that noise

I always hear (do you?) as the plane taxis
                    towards liftoff,
                    but I never bother

asking *what is that sound* when the pilot and I
                    come face-to-face
                    as we all deplane—

having jetted across time, finding ourselves
                    towed only by anticipation
                    of baggage we hope to claim.

IN 2016, THE AFRICAN-AMERICAN POET KYLE DARGAN IS ASKED TO CONSIDER WRITING MORE LIKE THE AFRICAN-AMERICAN POET ROSS GAY

Friends, will you bear with me today.
I noticed a man with no legs
wheeling over the deep
honeycomb joints
of the metro station's
platform. I began to pity
myself for being
one who must study
a paraplegic—the driving
rods his arms make
against the wheels—
before I am able
to choke down the ire
that tickles my throat lately,
before I begin, silently,
thanking the god
I've been taught to thank
for my able body.

That I *needed*
a legless man
to mirror what my
two working eyes
could have seen
explains maybe
my struggles with writing
for you, friends, a poem
about gratitude—gratitude
which is all the rave
now. Before
I might don any rage,

before the morning
newscast airs
white angst over
a lost country or the next
viral footage from a body
camera, before viewer
discretion has been advised,
you, friends, would like
that I first offer
thanks for the legs
and arms that have
not yet been taken
from me, thanks
for these last bits of earth
and what skin of mine
it has soiled.

My daybreak
inclination is to rise
with my mandible
locked by a functional
disillusionment
with our country—
a means of signifying
that requires no grace
be said before it devours
this buffet of civic failings.

My favorite poem
with gratitude
at its root is "Thanks"
by Yusef Komunyakaa.
In that slim lyric,
the gods are blind
and so he praises
off-mark bullets
and butterflies
that kept him alive

—kept his pilot
light lit despite
Vietnam's damp
futility. My imitation
would thank my mother,
who'd say to me *expect*
no kindness from The Man—
this despite how often
The Man was someone
she called *colleague,*
coworker, and *friend.*
Thanks, Mother,
for assuring my heart
never left its house
without pessimism's
cowl. I mean that.
It keeps me safe,
wards off the piercing
disappointment
like a thick winter
fabric that dulls chill.

Friends, you talk about joy.
You say *but there is*
joy, as if we must
convince you of this.
As if today's sharp air
will hang heavier and cleave
at your crown
if you don't know,
don't hear
from my lips, that I am
joyful. You want
my private aspect
(joy) to be public.
You want my public
aspect (pain) to be
stowed beneath

my bed like a precious
something someone
might steal from me.
But, listen now,
I am not a black church
with praise and thanks
rising off its roof in a harmony
you can hear from
the Sunday morning
safety of your home—
miles away
from any brick-
and-mortar black
church, unless we are
counting those bought
and spun into luxury
lofts on your blocks. Friends,

there is a reason
folk my age aren't singing
spirituals. You long
for an era you can't recall—
when my church
was public because privacy
was some off-the-books
currency only you could bank,
when everything about black
folk was forcibly accessible.
And though I now manage
some private space,
I'm still trying to buy
the same stitch of citizenship
you take for granted—
that you spill gimlets on,
sleep in, and leave crumpled
on your apartment floor.
I want that garment.

It would grant me
the warmth to live
as I am, unbundled, beyond
my small private space.
This is a sprawling
country, yet there is
so little of it I can bear
walking through
on my two full legs
without my mother's
heavy warning
woven on my shoulders.

You, friends, you will not
open yourselves to a tête-
à-tête about how you came
to possess that insulating
Americanness
you flaunt, but you
want me to open the doors
and let you inside
the small chapel
that is my joy. You want
to watch me there
on grateful feet
with grateful palms
opened to candlelight—
thankful. Yes, I am thankful,
but I cannot accommodate you
inside my gratitude.

Friends, I know you've come
for my private light,
to nestle in the shade
my grateful body casts.
But for you—if it is
only for you—I'll grant
my joy's flickering

no exposure. That's how close
I'll hug my candles. My joy
a refuge from a country
at times so cold
my hands don't feel the flame's
searing. You, friends—
you peckish for a peek
at my cloistered, incandescent
revelry—were you as earnest
about my frostbite, my burns,
I would have opened
these hands, sated you all.

ANOTHER POEM BEGINNING WITH A BULLET

My aunt is still alive—let us begin there instead—
and I step off the 34 Montclair into a breeze-
quelled dusk. Thanksgiving eve. It takes
twenty of my strides, or ten seconds, for the bus
engine belts' wheeze to dissipate. The hush
cracked by a pistol just before a getaway car tears
out the driveway of that lone, ill-zoned apartment
complex I loathe—its tall carcass, cop cars for flies.
I assume the gunners have seen me en route
to my mother's. I break—an Olajuwon pivot,
talking footwork—and I'm striding north
up Glenwood. Not too fast, not hinting I think
they know I've seen their make and plates,
their faces. And how many nights have I
juked through this city—an 8-bit millipede
chopping corners sharp so trouble could not trace
a path back to my mother's house?
Or how many nights, while Mother worked,
did I sleep over at my aunt's—defying lights-out
to play, blast those millipedes that lived inside
the gray Nintendo cartridge? Something shooting,
something crawling—always. I'm shuffling
towards my aunt's house, where millipedes
hid, where I hide until I can double back
—my neck unscrewed, head on swivel.
No one on the block keeps a porch light burning
except my mother, that yellow bug bulb
that now tints our veranda's canvas—there
a small Pollock reproduction in fresh blood.
And who walks over blood and then knocks?
But I do. I need to have my mother answer
the door, unharmed. It makes no difference
if I am announcing myself to a gunman,

for if that gun has already harmed my mother,
one more person would have to die—
the gunman or I. But she answers my knock.
Tells me how she opened the door for a man
who'd been held at gunpoint across the street.
He'd flinched just as the combustion I'd heard
expelled the bullet. With a grazed skull, he'd crawled
towards my mother's light at the same time as I fled.
The ambulance has come and gone, carrying him
down to the trauma center. The city no longer stops
at Mother's door. It has come inside now, has bled
here. In the living room. The night's long odds bend us
into slouching as we sit. But my aunt is alive,
and at tomorrow's feast I will see everyone. I will
remember this years later as one of the good days.

DISTances

I don't want to have to go through the fucking Middle Passage
to get to the new world.

—RAY JOSHUA

It is the night Michael Brown will be shot in Ferguson, Missouri, by an officer whose name will not be revealed for many days. I am eight hundred miles to the east in Washington, D.C., walking home with my friend Kirstyn from the Benning Road Metro Station. The quick route would take us up Texas Avenue into Benning Heights. A left turn on E Street would bring us to Alabama Avenue, and a right onto Alabama leads into a straight shot towards my house. That initial left turn on E Street would also bring us into the heart of the housing project still known as "Simple City" years after it earned infamy in the eighties and nineties as a drug strip and "crew" battlefield. Today still, the enclave is not to be slept on in that regard. From overhead or even from street level, the honeycomb of garden apartments—its denizens, its layout—would not look much different from the one where young Michael Brown will take six bullets and bleed for four hours into the street.

As Kirstyn and I begin to walk up Texas Avenue, a blazing convoy of police cruisers sweeps past us and up the hill. I assume—though I tell myself *I know*—where they are headed. By the time we arrive at the corner of Texas and E Street, I have already decided that we won't be making the aforementioned left turn. I've navigated enough nights when simple walks or bus rides through "the Ave" of Alabama have turned into police light exhibitions with cruisers and "paddy" vans barring foot and car traffic—blue-clad servants with guns searching for dread-headed youths, aiming to protect us from our own children.

The news of Michael Brown's shooting holds its breath—awaiting Kirstyn and me an hour in the future—but my eyes and ears have already ingested enough reasons for me to be wearied by scenes such as these.

"I'm not going up there—not tonight," I tell Kirstyn as she begins to pivot up E Street's sharp incline. "Let's keep going and cut over on Burns." The reroute adds ten minutes to the walk home. (It's the route I direct cabbies through to get to my house—particularly the ones who seem deathly afraid of transporting black folk into Southeast D.C. I even tip them extra as an enticement to accept the next fare that needs to get this way—and later on, I resent myself for rewarding their mere ability to treat me as though our fares and our humanity are equal to those who live downtown or uptown.)

Kirstyn and I walk in the street since Texas Avenue's sidewalk disappears for a few blocks following E Street—avoiding the Simple City projects for squat, deep-lotted homes mostly full of elderly and retired people. At Burns, we turn left and walk down the sparsely lit street. It's rare that I come across anyone after dark on Burns, but this night we do—a pair of sapling boys in "wifebeaters" whose skin blends into the evening's scrim.

Such after-dark encounters trigger specific processes in those who have grown up in what is casually referred to as the hood. Before even assessing if there is any threat potential, I must reckon how to appear unfazed and devoid of concern when I do eventually begin that assessment. No matter how rough one's neighborhood may be, to appear frightened only brings other condemnation. It is as though the community collective decrees *we all live here; we're all at risk, and do not think your concern for personal safety unique or precious.* Don't exhibit fear, but rather, project that you know what you will do—that you are reaction ready—in the event that some ruckus flares.

I temper my amble into a slightly sterner rhythm—but a rhythm nonetheless— and look towards the boys' hands and waists to see if there is any preparation for aggression. Then I pan up to see if they are communicating with each other. My brain's probability pistons fire rapidly—analyzing the environment like some cyborg's AI processor, though I am not a robot. I do know fear. But as all my impulses begin to settle into a program of action, as I feel my body tighten, I begin to accept how tired I am of feeling as though I have to treat these young boys as though they are our primary threats in the world. Yes, some of them pulled a gun on old Mrs. Outlaw and robbed her in the street. Yes, some carjacked the man who lives on Forty-Fifth (and likely regretted it as—him being an ex-con—he had little reservation about getting his gun and borrowing his mother's car to hunt them). Yes, some even tried to rob Mr. Purcell late one night only for him to snatch the gun from the boy's small hand before he could even attempt to squeeze off a scared round. All of that is true, but, as Mr. Purcell has proven, many of those who flirt with criminality are just young and scared—too shook to actually attempt to harm anyone who has survived this world much longer than have they.

I resolve, at age thirty-three, that I am no longer in the gray area between youth and adulthood—that in the physical and psychological battle for our community, I'm not a below radar neutral party. I'm on the same side as Mr. Purcell and Mrs. Outlaw. And though my assessment of the situation I am about to walk into suggests there is no certainty that these boys pose no threat, I decide that Kirstyn and I will walk right past them. If the two boys were Caucasian, I wouldn't even be engaged in this internal deliberation. That is also a useless point because the only pair of Caucasian men I've ever seen walk these streets are uniformed officers. I quietly pull my key chain from my pocket and tuck the serrated shaft of the longest sigil between my fisted index and middle finger.

Just as we approach the intersection where we will meet the boys on the other side, Kirstyn pulls my hand. "Come on. Let's cross the street." I do not feel relieved. In fact, I feel defeated as we cut diagonally through the street and the boys eye us. I see—no, I imagine—they are smirking. At the corner where we would have met them, the boys don't cross the street. They open the gate of the row house on the corner, then trot up the walkway and inside. They were merely trying to get home—just like Kirstyn and me, just like, for all we'll know, Michael Brown.

It has been three weeks since Officer Darren Wilson shot Michael Brown. I am preparing for a three-month trip back to the People's Republic of China, which seems less daunting now—like a release even—after many nights of shunning sleep to watch as indie journalists' iPhone broadcast the tumult on Florissant Avenue in Ferguson. It's nothing new for the police to kill a negro nor for the police to suppress—violently—negroes' unwillingness to peacefully accept the trampling of their rights, and my weariness flows from the deep awareness that neither is anything new. Except to many Caucasian people—particularly those who consider me a friend, who seem perplexed by the scowl I've taken to donning, revealing their blessed obliviousness to how treacherous it is for negroes—regardless of our individual lots—to live visibly or audibly as ourselves in this republic.

Kirstyn and I are listening to *On Point* while I try to shrink months' worth of appropriate garments down to one modest suitcase. Historian Jelani Cobb is Tom Ashbrook's guest on the radio show, and he and Ashbrook attempt to deepen what has been a mostly superficial public conversation about all that has transpired in Missouri over the past few weeks. When they reach the call-in segment of the show, I wait for the call that I know will come. And it comes, unsurprisingly, from the unrepentant South.

"James in Colombia, South Carolina," Ashbrook queues up the caller. "You're on with Jelani Cobb. James, thanks for calling."

James lets fly with his lament: "It always comes out to be that the white person is wrong. And if you look at Chicago and a lot of those other places, it's not the white police that are holding young black men down. It's the gangs that don't allow them to learn, to educate themselves, to go out and prosper . . . We're always blaming the white person, and young white kids are growing up thinking we're the worst people in the world, and that is not true."

Given how often "white" people have, in America's relatively short history, murdered or incited the murder of innocent black men and women, I find James's leading premise sadly amusing. Then I pause and suppose that I likely have—or have had at some point in time—friends just like him, for whom the most personally troubling aspect of these tragedies is that the outcry may be leading people who believe they are "white" to feel bad about who they fancy themselves to be. And as for the issue of growing children's sense of self, the question the moment seems to be asking is whether or not anyone can actually grow up while holding on to, cherishing, the idea that they are "white." At some point, a child must learn that the world does not revolve around him or her. But race continues to suggest that for "white" individuals, the world does in fact revolve around their perception of themselves. How else could one come to be concerned that in the aftermath of a negro male—barely on the cusp of adulthood and no longer posing a reasonable threat—being gunned down by law enforcement, it is incumbent upon the nation to ask if this moment is making "white" people think they are "bad"?

Ashbrook tosses James's question to Jelani Cobb—also informing him that he has only one minute for a rebuttal before the break. "It's going to take more than a minute," Cobb replies incredulously before conceding to the format and trusting Ashbrook's offer of more time on the other side of the station break.

Kirstyn chuckles into her cupped palm as I continue allotting myself pairs of underwear through the sponsor messages. "Oh my god," her phrasing much more forceful than her tone of voice. "That was so racist." I take the opportunity to say what I did not bother saying that night we crossed the street to avoid our idea of those two boys. "Maybe, but—I mean—is it that different than what we were thinking when we crossed that intersection that night?" I wait some beats before I continue—attempting to gauge whether or not she has taken any offense to my broaching the subject in this manner. "I mean, I didn't say anything because I know your concerns as a woman walking late at night are different than mine." I stop folding drawers. "I wasn't going to cross the street, but I didn't want to force you to go against your instincts either because—"

"But that's a reality here," she cuts me off. "You have fools out here that rob people. I've been robbed. I've had to stand there while a guy held a gun to my little brother's head. That's not me being afraid of someone because they're black. That's me being afraid of someone because they're here."

My initial impulse is to let her know that I too have had someone attempt to rob me—not in D.C. but back in East Orange, New Jersey—but I don't want to play "dueling traumas." I resent it when people do that to me, and our conversation merits something less strategic and more genuine.

"True," I respond. "True."

The bed becomes an expanse of unnavigable silence. We drift.

Neither of us remembered to listen for Cobb's response when the show returned from the break, though I already had little faith that any headway would be made—little faith not in Cobb but in the nation's ability to think about racialized violence as though history did not begin yesterday, as though the fears that have killed and continue to kill so many aren't buds on a well-crowned, toxic bush planted here not by nature nor by brown hands.

I wonder if negroes will ever get a sincere chance at shaping the popular American narrative as opposed to this existing within and in spite of it. I think about all the times I have tried to write a poem called "America: The Movie" but have never sincerely started—always finding myself overwhelmed by all the opportunities for retakes and alternative endings.

I click off the radio before the program ends and continue to pack—less concerned with what I may take with me, anticipating instead what I might get to leave behind.

CHINA CYCLE

Mao wanted to get rid of birds
because of the droppings;
then bugs took over and ate the trees.
—REETIKA VAZIRANI

I. ECONOMY CLASS

—United Flight 897, IAD to PEK

The woman had resisted for thirteen hours
before she began to vomit into the open
space between her ankles—her body crimped,
approaching the brace-for-impact posture.

Her face is now a tome of suffering.
Every wince another chapter. Every chapter
titled "It Is Hard to Be a Living Thing."

To be born human is to be tendered
this challenge to live larger than your woe.
And, no, there will not be reward nor rationale
beyond our pesky belief that this mortal meal
should be more than a mouthful of bitter seeds
that prime our innards' clenching—the purge
of what another day's survival has fed us.

II. DILEMMA IN COMPARISON

Ring cities, these sisters—D.C. and Beijing. The younger sibling

a chipped diamond inset within American democracy's asphalt
corona. The older has compounded its rings—think an elm,

thickening sapwood. The city that is a tree stretches—unpruned
towers grow to bark width and bough heights unfathomed

in D.C. There, lore claims no roof may rise above 1899's Building Act,
an untruth upholding Freedom's stance atop the Capitol as supreme—

her statue faced eastward, against Britain, so none forget
the diamond city's charred beginnings. Millennia of upheaval

are sown shallow in Beijing, where our handlers direct our gaze
up towards new leaves. My eyes seek Beijing's trunk—its girth

gnarled and reaching. I want to see how an empire seat survives
not war but the cost of living's steady siege. Should one hope

for dollars green or for saws to slice through constricting rings?

III. BODY BINHAI

—Tianjin, Binhai New Area

A two-hour, dead-road drive south
to where New Binhai's bones await
their marrow—the country-
women and countrymen
who will be drawn from the hills
and fields to raise the blood
volume in the body.

Like a fictive species, this New
Binhai is more idea, a skeleton
of national aspirations
wrapped with transported earth
—each design far greater than
what will be made of the cured
and brittle grains of soil, concrete.

Its gullet opens to Yellow Sea—
its giant steel tongues lap up
what cargo barges haul into the bay.

Its diet is one of an industrial
omnivore. Binhai bleeds gross
domestic product's nutrients.

But New Binhai is a body in stasis
without its marrow, which
cannot be mined nor harvested.

It strives to be known as the Middle
Kingdom's third sun, to unseat Hong Kong—
an ascension the Party has decreed.

And the transplant will commence
regardless of who pulses in the hills,
what lineage the State-flooded graves unmoor.

V. A PROGRESSIVE MILE

—Binhai Athletic Field
Shanghai Dao and Zhongxin Lu

I step past the English sign—SMOKELESS STADIUM—
and find a bench, where I begin changing
into my shoes. I run in neon-orange Nikes,
fashioning my feet as sparks off the rust track.

Sundown, and the lanes are full—fifty or more
walkers, maybe six runners. My first loop
outpaces the joggers—the warm-up
lap when my nerves cross-check my body
before transmitting the go-ahead to my heart.

My gait lengthens through the second lap—
becoming a gallop as I lose sense of my own dark
spectacle here. My eyes forward, gazing into
that space my coaches' shouts never pierced
(up thirty degrees, where I see only figures
before me, and nothing exists in my periphery).

Seven thousand miles from home, the 1600m
still burns at the same point—third lap when pain
arrives like a wounded devil you may refuse.
(I pull his weight upon my back, crank quicker strides.)

For the last lap, I ask my muscles, *What do we have*
faster than this—awaiting a response as I cross
the twelve-hundred-meter line. There I promise
my feet they may rest when next we touch this mark.
Then I sprint through my abdomen's unraveling.

A trotted cooldown lap, then back to the bench.
While I stretch and replace my simple black slip-ons,
I'm joined by a man who sits, lights a cigarette,
and silently gazes at me through smoke—unflinching
in the corner of my eye. After three minutes, I greet him.
The shock of my "ni hao" cracks his stare—that of a man
caught surveying a foreign car with no concern for currency
conversion, fancying all he'd do behind the wheel.

VII. NI, WO

Though rain falls sulfuric
in Tianjin, it is said some long
for showers—for a drizzling
excuse to share a hip
with another warm body

underneath an umbrella.
Affection here has seemed
a much-cloistered thing
—a pair practically needing
pretext to press

so close in public. Our translators
regale us with this story:
nascent lovers on a stroll,
so shyly enthralled—yen
cocooned within each's own
guts—that when one trips
and tumbles down a street vent,
the other walks on ahead,
too far for the fallen's voice to reach.
It was thought the epitome
of romance.

      A downpour
clears the star-gold
transit buses off the street.
I slosh home, pondering
how strong would be the charge
of two bodies' willing array
beneath a meager, black umbrella—
their current quickening
this dark, wet circuit of a city.

IX. THE WAY OF INTERSECTIONS

Let the dragonfly
    teach you how one
        can cross wisely
    where two Binhai
roads make a junction.
    Dragonfly—a blur of stained-
        glass wings perched on air
    until curiosity's
winds carry its hovering
    upon you. The approach
        may at first appear
    predatory. Ignore
your instincts. It hungers
    not for your blood,
        but for your blood
    within the mosquito.
Its flight path will bank
    before reaching your skin—
        only flirtation with
    your motion, nothing more.
Remember this
    when you venture
        a stride onto the pavement
    of the right turn lane.
Like the dragon-
    fly, any sky-blue
        cab or red moped
    owns the right-of-way.
They may honk,
    feign a desire
        to mow you down.
    Just move forward.
They will swarm.
    They will not sting.

X. THE SHOUTS OF TANGGU STATION

My weak ear for the lilts of Mandarin
speech does not spare me. I hear

the parched yowls mouthed by the indigent
old man bedded on Tanggu Station's stairwell.

"Meiguo, meiguo," he groans—lifting his beggar's
bowl without a "qing wen" or "dui bu qi." He is not blind.

Still, I wonder how he knows I am no Ethiopian,
Dominican, Caribe, or any of the other bloods

my skin is oft mistaken to carry back in the States.

While I weave through the clouds of grilling
squid outside the Tanggu entrance, a boy leans out,

halloes from his car, "Aye, amigo!" I nod, relented
to his eagerness. Why bother working the loom

of cerebral lobes, weaving the phrase "Bu *amigo*.
Wo shi meiguo ren"? I'm so far from believing

our voices might merge like highway Jin Tang's
traffic. On the walk home, I stop for practice paper. "Xie xie,"

I thank the shopkeeper. "Xie xie *ni*," she corrects me.

The hanzi for "hai" (海) I decipher from expressway
signs above us as we depart the new Port of Binhai.

I ask Dongxia what "Shanghai" then means.
"No meaning. When it is name, it is just name."

I struggle to swallow her response. I've noticed
the semantics of Mandarin's myriad characters

harbors the figurative—how "holy" as hanzi
stacks the character for "other" atop the arboreal

character for "earth," resculpting the metaphor
in calligraphy (圣). I show Dongxia my strokes

for a character that's caught my eye (京) to ask,
again, for translation. "This means Beijing—

one character." But "bei" I've now memorized
as "north." I follow my finger through my glossary

until it catches on "jing": "capital." North Capital.
Beijing—as much a name as a geographical

distinction. Later, I glean "shang" (上) off street
signs near my lodging. I open the dictionary,

which confesses it means "up," maybe "upper."
Upper Port. Shanghai. North of Hong Kong.

(I plan to tell Dongxia there was a duke
of an old English York. The York that now cradles

Manhattan is the New. I seek similar histories
when I ask what hides behind the hanzi's blades.)

Before I fancy myself a sleuth of language
here in the Middle Nation (中国), I must learn

what I mean in Mandarin. After calling myself
"meiguo" (美国) for weeks, I realize that

it can't be simply "America." My book confides
that "mei" means beautiful, that I am "ren"

(人) from the Beautiful Country. I bemoan
the translation, yet I was not brought here

to explain all the beauty not found at home.

XII. EARLY ONSET SURVIVOR'S GUILT

For the fifth morning consecutive, Binhai is unwilling
to remove its headpiece of haze. A quarter mile
beyond my window—no hope of seeing skyline—I know
there is a city, one whose sidewalks I have trod,
one inhaling its own particulate erasure.
In two weeks' time, I'll be over this nation, atop it rather
—buckled in as our plane breaches the floating matte
moat that often estranges eastern China's ground
dwellers from the open sky. The engines' hum
will not smother my ears' memories of modest people's
chronic cough-and-spit throughout the day.
I pine for the cloud-daubed atmosphere back home
—the panorama my eyes knit when they lift
towards the Washington Monument's stabbing apex.
I am not lamenting inflamed lungs nor
the soot to which many here resign themselves—
an impasse between gritty air and the capillaries
that hug alveoli. Where there is sadness,
it bubbles from thoughts of the blue
that awaits me, the blue I take for granted, the blue
I never asked to be born beneath. But I have seen it—
that blue whose weeks-long absence here renders
a sky little more than a mirror of decay.

XV. VOICES ON THE RIVER

6:00 A.M. or some days the bitter hour before,
they climb the long, low slope of stairs that crest
gray floodwalls flanking the Haihe. Their solo
or paired heels lock onto the boardwalk planks,
before belting a sequence of hollers—maybe words—
difficult to discern through their amplitude.

For lone voices in a city of fourteen million,
they fill the grainy emptiness around high exhaust
stacks between Hebin Park and Dengshan'gu reservoir.

Here, circular dining tables and a choreographed
surge of cranes all echo the *harmony* developers
and spokeswomen tout. But then are there
these men who wake ahead of the roosters
so they can bellow over the growth, over freighters,
and towards Bohai Bay. They answer
to an impulse other than the mitotic
grind of a national plan. Something primal.
A singular drive unsnyced while the city continues
to breed crowds that dance and sing on schedule.

So who are these who venture to disrupt? They call
back to waves—lost seabirds pruning sooty
wings, awash in recollection of water, unbossed.

XVI. THE WOODEN PHOENIX AT LING TONG

None of the skeletal grounds-keeping crew
can recount how the bird found itself
trapped within the tree, but the wood-carver's
intuition told him to dig for the phoenix
where rot takes to heartwood.
The fanning roots' knots unearthed
along with the stump, the carver
washed and scraped those vessels
free of dirt—ceasing the tree's
communion with the soil.

Now buffed and varnished, they blaze.

The carver gouged into the trunk's
nub. Bark split (like the bodhisattva
Guanyin's head and arms
when she tried to reach,
to comprehend, the suffering
of all still cycling through samsara).
Strips of wood gave way, and in time,
the peacock phoenix began
to emerge. The carver chiseled
eyes within six feathers—trusting
negative spaces between the roots

would account for the remaining
nine thousand nine hundred
and ninety-four retinas—their gaze
exponential, transmuting evil
into sublimity. But before the phoenix
could fly, its breast and wings
had to taste varnish too, and the burning
bird could not escape becoming art.

The carver? His hands, his eyes
have since vanished with the rest of his flesh—
becoming air (feeding our fire) like a god.

XX. DA SHUO

On the other side of the great firewall, the Uyghur Tohti has lost his free life to sentencing with no testimony. Hong Kong nights glimmer with the glow of smartphone faces turned torches in demonstrators' hands. The financial district, its party-tight tycoons, illuminated. The world can see—the world bent to English. Thus I can see. Yet the hanzi here behind the wall cannot align themselves into news of unrest. Unlike America. So much news there that knowing—or caring—is uncouth. Behind this wall, Tianjin's pedestrians pass or smack flush into each other with no knowledge that officials have canceled the National Day fireworks in Hong Kong. Fireworks' news travels widely here. How you hear the human fabric unravel and restitch on this censored side of the wall. A single barrage: a wedding. Two blasts separated by a pause: a funeral. You will not hear the country outgrowing its tailored harmony. (A sound I know from home.) Protesting students have their Instagram eyes gouged out. Unlike with words, there is no subtle way to sanitize the world web's imagebrain. Panoramas of skyscrapers—thirty at a time—rise on this side of the wall. Putin grips Xi standing next to the Next Big Thing on this side of the wall. Rows of dark-suit apparatchiks fold themselves into a mitochondrion on this side of the wall. China Central Television broadcasts the first fifteen channels on this side of the wall, and small women styled with identical bob cuts sit at the anchor desks—words, like quick-setting mortar, pour calmly from their lips.

XXI. MEAL AT PYONGYANG

Not trusted with stove or icebox at our lodging,
we develop a habit of dining Korean—its familiar
grilled meat, less grease than some Shandong fare.

The businessman who Seongah befriended in flight
over the Yellow Sea recommends traditional Chinese
opera then a meal downtown. "We are now inside

North Korea," she jests once we're all seated
at the restaurant administered by Pyongyang—
owned by middlemen who must remit USD.

Hospitable, though stiff, the servers dish kimchi.
A waitstaff of all young women dressed in classic
Joseon-ot bell-cut skirts—imported children

of ranking apparatchiks. With smiles, they serve us
then turn down dark halls, their brows sunken.
What has drawn us? These waitresses, renowned

for trading trays for microphones and breaking
into patriotic ballads. But we are tonight's only patrons—
the city's Korean diners having been drained

by the Chinese holiday. "No show this evening,"
we are informed midmeal. "I'm sorry
we won't get to hear your song," Seongah laments

to the woman who clears our table—the diva,
unbeknownst to us. Maybe the exchange
rate on otherness affords us an exception. As we finish,

strobe light streams into our side dining room,
while the ticks of sound check replace the North
Korean newscaster's grim drone. Warned against

photography, we emerge into a production. Our bus girl
belle now the lead vocalist in a trio that harmonizes
and pirouettes before an unmanned rhythm section—

their backing a karaoke track. Perplexed cashiers,
cooks creep into the hall from the edges, observing us
observing them. "What's wrong," someone asks me,

noting my head turned from the stage. "I have a thing
about compulsory art." The waitresses take their solos,
including an accordion medley to rile our Polish friend.

Then the truncated set in the empty hall ends. We clap.
They ask when will we return. We invite them to Binhai.
One whispers that they are watched and cannot leave.

XXII. DEVILS HAVE NO FANS

Their shirts say *I Wish You Were*
Hero, say *Cock Whore*, say *Open*
Your Mind, say *Fuck Off*. Graphic
tee vocabulary likely surplused
from unsold stock in the West, freighted
east. O, the allure of exotic language,
the catharsis of cussing. Should I
laugh as they do when my misspoken
tone turns "cat" (猫) into "hair" (毛),
risk assuming they do not know
what their clothes profess? "Hello,"
a teenage boy chirps one night
along the bund—waiting, per usual
fashion, until we are five yards past.
"Die, motherfucker," he growls at ten.
It is surely something he learned
from Hollywood, our action flicks—
what he knows heroes say coolly
before they blow we villains to bits.

Dear Echo

Let the earth be the thing that takes you apart.
—FRANCINE J. HARRIS

NATURAL CAUSES

Naturally, the gun is purchased from a farm in Virginia—pulled from a bushel of barrels by a tremulous hand, a young man's. His other fist proffers sweat-wilted dollars. The farmer, compensated, keeps his gaze down so as to remember nothing of the boy's face. A young face is another young face. His customers rarely return older. Seasons matter little to him—none of the guns he sells are grown from seed. Each a plug he tends only until maturity, harvest. Naturally, he will not smell the fused aroma of sulfur and specters escaping the bodies of the boys this boy will smoke upwind, upriver. In D.C. In Prince George's. Leaves burn where the farmer lives. Deer and turkeys hunted, but never with the pistols he sells to these boys who trade fire with boys. Many of them will not live to see any creature of the woods, though their dumped corpses may share the woods with the deer and the turkeys. And the leaves. Every year the leaves bury memory of those juvenile graves—the crackling umbers and rusts muting to umbrage what otherwise should be rage.

SUBLIMATION

Grant me this obsession: any image
depicting an entity as it disappears—
            stock-still vanishings
        that seem far
different than cardiac arrest,
different than the plasma
                        rivers   within
that draw parched,   mud-cracked.
A pure fish needs not water nor blood.
Everything in the universe is already
        swimming, or clinging
to some dark matter raft.   Or so I am told.
Or so I observe as I study a sketch
of a horse galloping
            into shapelessness—its head
and neck becoming coral   then sand
then emptied   space. The horse has not been
dispelled. The horse is substantiated
across the page and beyond
        the framing black, its bits
corralled at last by my inhales. Do I become
the horse? One answer:
what of us is not related through sublimation
—the phase matter enters when it grows
weary of holding
                    form? I am tired. I want to be
worthy of an alternative undoing
to which I might surrender—
another atomic process,
        a dissolution
more ecstatic than decomposition,
to punctuate my clearing
                        sigh.

My kinetic flesh
relinquished for the uncolored, odorless,
tasteless ubiquity of a vapor.

SEPARATING

there is blood in the morning egg
that makes me turn and weep
—AUDRE LORDE

Between the work at work and the work at home, I rush
inside a grocery to buy the bits for quick breakfasts

that leave me hungry by the time I return to my office.
It is an organic market, and as I shop I can hear my mother—

her mouth full of pennies—mocking each cent I overpay
for staples. But time's expense burns black holes in pockets,

so no detour to a cheaper store. So honey priced like wine.
So six eggs for what would buy twelve. All in the name

of time. It will be days before I have a moment when I can
pause my pre-commute to click on the electric kettle, boil

water for steeping rooibos and poaching eggs. Eventually,
I reach inside the refrigerator, revisit the words "cage-free"

"pasture-raised" which, in my earlier haste, read like gibberish
strings of dollar signs. When I crack open the brown pods,

what glops into the ramekin is a yolk-yellow so plump and lucent.
I tear up thinking of all the weak or sallow suns I have dropped

into water, of the stressed existences that made those eggs.
What of my thin shell or my own yoke unbroken within me

(both functions of money, time, deficits)? And I know nothing
about industrial farms. And I understand so much of blackness

as what I do in spite of my caging. But I know I cannot buy
another egg not laid by a bird I believe foraged, walked freely

under the sun—deciding how to value her motion, her blood.
A bourgeois privilege, I know. But if not to make that choice,

why else am I grinding myself down for these wages?

GENERATION KINDLING

> *Youth full of fire ain't got nowhere to go.*
> —ANDRÉ BENJAMIN

Near woods' edge, the boy kneels

        to pry up the caps and flick matches

down oil lines of foreclosed homes.

        Wind drag snuffs the flames before

each charred match head plunks

        against the sludge-slick

bends in the pipes. The boy fails

        the tests at school, where some

say he needs an outlet, a father,

        therapy. The boy: the incarnate

will of the forest—those jack pines

        that desire a blaze vehement

and swift before their serotinous

        cones open, letting seeds

reach the rich bed of scorched needles.

        The pines would prefer a wildland

fire, something felicitous as lightning

        lighting underbrush into pyre—

updrafts awash with flame. But we are

        too quick—with our helicopters,

retardant, trench lines, and

        pretorching. Our intent to contain.
Thus the forest birthed the boy—

        a fruit with flesh like our own rather than
rosined scales. And were we so busy

        making the boy promises (*if you are*
a pious boy, a quiet boy, a still boy),

        no one noticed how his irises darkened
in the fall or how the spring

        breeze made a music as it wrapped
around him? All the bourgeois

        bits and trappings dangled for his obedience
will be out of reach in the coming seasons.

        We know that. The boy can sense
our default. So instead, he now seeks

        the inferno coded within himself.
He is not the only one the pines

        have sown among us, and we will see
smolder before we peg his many siblings.

        Absorbed with saving our hides, our own
ephemeral futures, we imagine

        ourselves stewards. We keep
our lives green—preventing fires

        when the forest wants to burn.

TREDEGAR

—RICHMOND

Black dragonflies chase away
their red cousins. *Just the law of things
here*—my lay naturalist logic
for ecosystem, pecking order. See?
I understand. The river fish
(*Pylodictis olivaris* a lithograph
will later teach me), they retreat
beneath invasive patches of hydrilla
as I approach the James's shallow
water column. Big suckers—
I wager instinct beseeches them
to seek shelter from the shadows
of larger suckers like me. I suppose
that's how the day triggers out here,
until it doesn't—until I notice
one of those sleek, fat bodies
cleave free from the current
to snatch a dragonfly off the river's
skin. I see my rippled reflection:
I am the stupid human. My eye
unable to distinguish hiding
from lurking—each a form
of stillness. I failed to set them apart
until the catfish's jaws snapped
and mashed the water dipper's wings.

THIRTY-FOUR

The cypress trees I planted after
I bought the dead woman's house
sway higher than me, even taller
than the out-of-work chimney.
And the neighbor, Ms. Miller, who
watched me wedge up crepe myrtles
in favor of then knee-high evergreens,
she has died. The stressed myrtles
withered but lived once replanted
in a hedgerow behind the Japanese maple.
I drenched them daily. Now they sing
a steady emerald harmony
backing the maple's burgundy croon.

Yes, there are days, say today, when
I am fine suspending here my journey

of breathing—not a fatal capitulation.
Just ready. When questions of *what more*
arise, only wind, only wind. Ambition,
though, remains an antagonizing allergen,
and my body secretes will's mucus
throughout my day's work. I never learned
from Charles Wright the sage way a poet
pulls poems out of their somber descents.
Maybe I'm not yet sufficiently worn
by this world. (*Not old enough,*
what everyone tells me.) But explain that
to my palms, to my soles, to these cypress
fronds that fan above me, blatant
in their surprise that I am still here.

THE DARKENING

A murder of crows for the many
whose blood vessels will be shred
by barrel bombs' shrapnel—the intent to maim
without exclusion. A murder of crows
for each mother and father who pawns all
except what will cover their backs
so they might join the thousands
driven into exasperated seas
to shirk their turn at becoming
casualties. A murder of crows
for the tiny bodies those seas swallow.
And do you see? A murder
of crows for those of us with eyes
keen yet uncurious. A murder of crows
for those who cooperate
and are slaughtered nonetheless.
And do you see the sky? A murder of crows
for those well aware of how easily
rights to a homeland can be voided
by militias adorned with flags and royal
rifles. A murder of crows for those
who have never worn a uniform but have
had war waged against them. A murder
of crows for a uranium pact feared fragile.
A murder of crows for the airmen who study
display screens on an armed force base,
waiting to tap drone triggers that incinerate
faces in another hemisphere. A murder
of crows for the downed pilot—his parachute
guiding him into a lake where he is rescued
then burned alive for the camera. And do you see
the sky feathering in iridescent, dark—
how it does not resemble the sky you know?

It is the only sky the many have seen
for years. What little light in condolences
you offer—you, like it or not,
born with bread in your fists,
born adorably feeding the crows
the way your father fattened the crows
and his father fattened the crows. When
the murders of crows arrive broad
as a giant black stork, they claw apart
the hospitals, the nesting beds.
They bundle the last obstetrician in rubble
then soar up to perch above
the scrum, blocking the sunlight.
When the first mother abandoned during labor
breaks—when her bloody yolk runs
and makes a mud of all the dust—no longer
is there a murder. A birth: the debris and rust
tinged clay shape themselves into an unforgiving
mountain—a new scar we give the Earth's
flesh. And sometimes a scar
marks healing. And sometimes a scar can
only remind you what burned, what was
severed, what had to flee
a body—to be beheld never again.

DEAR ECHO

I know the planet Earth is 'bout to explode.
Kind of hope that no one saves it.
We only grow from anguish.
    —MAC MILLER

In the likely event of galactic calamity—
our sun's hydrogen reserves fused through,
the star-turned-red-giant bloating
as do our corpses—you will require flames.
Between the solar shockwave and Earth's
rattling—an opaque interval—you must
watch, but we people prior will have left
no crude fluid for ignition, for light,
having tapped this rock to gorge
our bellies to petroleum ache.
Perhaps you will have evolved—blood
supplemented with Edison and Tesla's
currents, half your body fed by generators
that slow cure your biomass or waste.
Maybe you will be self-luminous.

      But if you are still—like we,
like me—a mere meat pod fated to watch
Mercury and Venus engulfed, surely
you hold designs for an interplanetary ark.
Anticipate humanity's years spent
adrift in the dark liquor of space—lost
within hibernation and missing mother-
planet, further estranged from all
revelation of how we came to be.

From this unproven vantage point (inside
our history with no solid alpha), I claim to pity
your inherited task—to catalog the last
telluric pulse, close the case of "man" as now

known. But beneath my softened hide,
I'm envious. All of our missteps as shepherds,
all the graffiti eclipsing our souls, all of it
will cinder and you will view this erasure
from your Mars-bound barge. You will know
the phenomenon that is judgment, see it real time
as prophets allegedly witnessed. Sapiens will never
have beheld a clearer beacon to be reborn—

In one of the many publishing positions I held in my twenties, before settling into full-time teaching, I worked with an editor who thoroughly did not care for Nikky Finney's work. There was a particular pleasure, it seemed, the editor savored at any opportunity to deride or deny her writing. I had been reading and internalizing Nikky Finney for years—her second collection, *Rice*, being my first encounter—but the editor's criticisms were so insistent that I began to wonder if I wasn't reading closely enough. (That happens. Works we think are wise in our early engagement with deep reading become less so as we outgrow them.) But I never found that to be the case, so that editor and I agreed to disagree, or rather I came to an agreement with myself to keep my mouth clamped.

It often feels to me as though whatever recent year just passed was the year that *Head Off & Split* won the National Book Award. Not that it was very long ago, but that moment remains of particular significance to me as in the years between my experiences with that editor and the moment of her recognition, I'd come to know Nikky Finney as one of those who are most diligent and humble among writers—a warrior-monk who "prays" and practices her craft with the tenacity of someone who remembers, still tastes and smells, the intimate and international wars waged to keep people like her from becoming such apostles of language. Nikky Finney's model of being able to live off the land until one creates the undeniably worthy work, to then stand up in the bright lights but ultimately return to melancholy coves of writing, has taught me so much about persistence. When I think of the dismissal of her work that I personally witnessed and then see or hear from her now, I can believe how cheap the poe-biz is in comparison with the miracle of creative integrity and dedication. I likely would not still be doing this (publishing, not writing) without her model, and I feel blessed to now share a press with her.

This book doesn't happen without poet and editor Parneshia Jones, who I would say is not only a talented seer of poetry but also a genius of placing faith in poets. Her effect on the literary world is becoming increasingly undeniable. This actual manuscript grew out of my working with Erika Stevens (on a new and selected I thought I need to be properly *seen* as a poet), whose vision for book projects always nudges my own to more meaningful goals. Kwame Dawes's merciless eye was an invaluable impetus to push me to push the poems to do more, as was Bettina Judd's questioning. My colleagues Lily Wong and Rachel Louise Snyder also provided feedback without which I could not have confidently released this book into the world. My sincere thanks to all of them.

To my D.C. workshopping group who saw and spoke back to these poems (Sandra Beasley, Christopher Greggs, Ailish Hopper, Daria-Ann Martineau, Elizabeth Lindsey Rogers, Maureen Thorson), much appreciation. Many of you are in different places now (as is often the case with those who live in Washington, D.C.), but I still see you and your work.

And thank you to the generous and hospitable Chinese Writers Association for inviting me back to China—this time Tianjin—and continuing the creative exchange between our nations. My city and my home will always be a welcoming destination for your writers.

Book epigraphs: James Baldwin quoted from his speech given at the University of California, Berkeley, January 15, 1979. Trugoy the Dove aka Dave Jolicoeur quoted from the lyrics of "Ego Trippin' (Part Two)" off De La Soul's album *Buhloone Mindstate* (Tommy Boy, 1993).

"Dark Humor" section epigraph: Richard Pryor quoted from the track "Bicentennial Nigger," off his comedy album of the same title (Warner Bros., 1976).

"Daily Conscription": James Baldwin quoted from the aforementioned speech given at the University of California, Berkeley.

"Looking East as a Man Repairs Lights on the South Street Pier": Walt Whitman quoted from the poem "Crossing Brooklyn Ferry," as published in *Leaves of Grass* (1867).

"Death Toll": Barack Obama quoted from his statement in response to the shootings at Umpqua Community College, October 1, 2015.

"Eastland": Yasiin Bey quoted from the lyrics to "Grown Man Business," off his sophomore album *The New Danger* (Rawkus, 2004).

"La Petite Mort": Fatimah Asghar quoted from Twitter, February 18, 2016.

"Dave Chappelle Confuses George Washington with Thomas Jefferson": George Washington quoted from a letter written to Edward Rutledge, May 5, 1789. Dave Chappelle (italics) quoted from his 2004 stand-up special *For What It's Worth*.

"In 2016, the African-American Poet Kyle Dargan Is Asked to Consider Writing More Like the African-American Poet Ross Gay": Opening line taken from Ross Gay's poem "Catalog of Unabashed Gratitude," from his collection of the same title (University of Pittsburgh Press, 2015).

"Distances" section epigraph: Ray Joshua (played by Saul Williams) quoted from the motion picture *Slam* (Trimark, 1998).

"China Cycle" section epigraph: Reetika Vazirani quoted from the poem "Beijing," in *World Hotel* (Copper Canyon Press, 2002).

"Dear Echo" section epigraph: francine j. harris quoted from episode two of the *All Up in Your Ears* podcast, May 2016.

"Separating": Andre Lorde quoted from the poem "Parting," as published in *The Black Unicorn* (W. W. Norton, 1995).

"Generation Kindling": André Benjamin quote taken from the lyrics to "Gasoline Dreams," off OutKast's fourth studio album, *Stankonia* (LaFace, 2000).

"Dear Echo": Mac Miller quoted from the lyrics to "Friends," off his 2014 mixtape *Faces*.

A note on Mandarin Chinese usage: As acknowledged in the poems, I struggled with capturing—hearing or speaking—the range of tones in the Chinese language. (Though, for a short time, I felt better after a taxi driver in Binhai explained to me that he could not understand the speech of someone giving us directions because that person was from southern China and intoned as such.) The pinyin in this book thus lacks tonal accents as an intentional means of representing the unfortunate "flatness" of my experience with the language, though learning and writing hanzi offered some respite. My hope is that without the accents (which are essential for distinguishing the myriad homonyms), the context allows readers to access what the pinyin communicates in various instances.